D1607175

PowerKiDS
Readers

SEA FRIENDS
LOS AMIGOS DEL MAR

SEA OTTERS
LAS NUTRIAS MARINAS

SAM DRUMLIN
TRADUCCIÓN AL ESPAÑOL: EDUARDO ALAMÁN

PowerKiDS
press™

New York

Published in 2013 by The Rosen Publishing Group, Inc.
29 East 21st Street, New York, NY 10010

First Edition

Editor: Amelie von Zumbusch
Book Design: Colleen Bialecki and Liz Gloor   Traducción al español: Eduardo Alamán

Photo Credits: Cover Patrick Endres/Visuals Unlimited/Getty Images; p. 5 Neelsky/Shutterstock.com; p. 7 Heather A. Craig/Shutterstock.com; p. 9 Pyma/Shutterstock.com; pp. 11, 13, 17, 19 iStockphoto/Thinkstock; p. 15 Marc Moritsch/National Geographic/Getty Images; p. 21 Karen Kasmauski/National Geographic/Getty Images; p. 23 Mark Newman/Photo Researchers/Getty Images.

Library of Congress Cataloging-in-Publication Data

Drumlin, Sam.
  [Sea otters. English & Spanish]
Sea otters = Las nutrias marinas / by Sam Drumlin ; translated by Eduardo Alamán. — 1st ed.
    p. cm. — (Powerkids readers: sea friends = Los amigos del mar)
Includes index.
ISBN 978-1-4488-9976-0 (library binding)
1. Sea otter—Juvenile literature. I. Title. II. Title: Nutrias marinas.
QL737.C25D7518 2013
599.769'5—dc23
                                            2012022557

Web Sites: Due to the changing nature of Internet links, PowerKids Press has developed an online list of Web sites related to the subject of this book. This site is updated regularly. Please use this link to access the list: www.powerkidslinks.com/pkrsf/otter/

Manufactured in the United States of America

CPSIA Compliance Information: Batch #W13PK3: For Further Information contact Rosen Publishing, New York, New York at 1-800-237-9932

CONTENTS

CONTENIDO

Sea otters are smart!

¡Las nutrias marinas son muy listas!

They live in the Pacific Ocean.

Viven en el Océano Pacífico.

They live near the coast.

Viven cerca de la costa.

They have thick **fur**.

Tienen **pelaje** espeso.

It keeps out water.

El pelaje las mantiene secas.

Sea otters eat mostly shellfish.

Las nutrias marinas comen mariscos.

They use rocks to break
open shells.

Usan rocas para abrir
las conchas.

They eat a lot.

Las nutrias comen mucho.

A group of sea otters is a **raft**.

A un grupo de nutrias se le llama **manada**.

Babies are **pups**.

Sus bebés son **cachorros**.

23

WORDS TO KNOW / PALABRAS QUE DEBES SABER

fur / (el) pelaje

pup / (el) cachorro

raft / (la) manada

INDEX

ÍNDICE